D1458953

Stories

Tish Farrell

Your writing quest

Artificial Intelligence, genetic engineering, probes on Mars –
where is our technology taking us? To a sun-bright future or
planet collapse? If questions like these fire your imagination,
then learn how to turn them into stunning science-fiction
stories. This book cannot transport you to another galaxy, but
it will help chart your course on a voyage of discovery – to
write beyond the limits of the known world.

Your mission, then, is to find new ways of probing an alien
environment, otherwise known as the Hidden Depths of Your
Imagination. To help you on your way, there will be a variety
of training and brainstorming exercises that will develop your
creative writing skills. There will also be plenty of examples
from famous science-fiction writers to inspire you. The voyage
to discovering your writing skills will not always be easy. It
could take light-years.

But remember, with science fiction, the sky is NEVER the
limit. There are always new dimensions to explore.

Good luck!

Copyright © ticktock Entertainment Ltd 2006
First published in Great Britain in 2006 by ticktock Media Ltd.,
Unit 2, Orchard Business Centre, North Farm Road, Tunbridge Wells, Kent, TN2 3XF
We would like to thank: Shobha Mucha for her help with this book.
ISBN 1 86007 923 7 PB
Printed in China
A CIP catalogue record for this book is available from the British Library.

CONTENTS

How to Use This Book   4

INTRODUCTION

Why do Writers Write?   6

CHAPTER 1: Getting Started

First Things First   8
• *Writing materials* • *Writing places*
• *Writing zones*

The Writing Habit   10
• *Training* • *Reward yourself*

The Reading Habit   12
• *Reading* • *What is Sci-Fi?* • *Read widely*
• *Themes* • *Taking notes*

CHAPTER 2: Writing styles and ideas

A Writer's Voice   14
• *Find your voice* • *Experiment*

Finding Ideas   16
• *Ideas search* • *Don't panic!* • *Freeing your stories*
• *Research* • *Where to look*

How to Create a Landscape   20
• *Discover a setting* • *Laying down the law*
• *World building*

Using Words to Create Worlds   22
• *Don't go OTT* • *Convincing settings* • *Defined threats*

CHAPTER 3: Creating Characters

Heroes   24
• *Finding a hero* • *Names* • *Strengths and weaknesses*

Villains   26
• *Types of villains* • *Motivation for evil*

The Supporting Cast   28
• *The cast* • *Creating characters* • *Magical companions*

CHAPTER 4: Viewpoint

Who's Speaking?   30
• *All-seeing view* • *Third person*
• *Multiple viewpoint*

CHAPTER 5: Synopses and Plots

Ready to Write   32
• *Blurbs* • *Synopses* • *Story maps* • *Scenes* • *Themes*
• *Inspiration* • *Novels* • *Short stories*

Good Beginnings   36
• *Dramatic beginnings* • *Starting points*

Unmuddled Middles   38
• *False endings* • *Action* • *Problems* • *Challenge the reader*

Gripping Endings   40
• *Choosing an ending* • *Wrapping up* • *Intrigue* • *Twists*

CHAPTER 6: Winning Words

Making Words Work   42
• *Imagery* • *Rhythm and length* • *Mood changes*

CHAPTER 7: Scintillating Speech

Creating Dialogue   44
• *Evesdropping* • *Convention* • *Importance of dialogue*
• *Viewpoints* • *Maintain momentum* • *Evoke emotion*
• *Invent language* • *Accents* • *Keep in character*

CHAPTER 8: Hints and Tips

Beating Writing Problems   50
• *Insecurities* • *The writing habit* • *Criticism* • *Fresh ideas*
• *Don't get stuck*

More Tricks of the Trade   52
• *Writer's block* • *Rebuild your characters*
• *Role play* • *Journals*

CHAPTER 9: Finishing touches

Preparing Your Work   54
• *Editing* • *Titles* • *Be professional* • *Books* • *Covers*

Reaching an Audience   56
• *Publishing* • *Writing clubs* • *Finding a publisher*
• *Writer's tip*

CHAPTER 10: What Next?

When You've Finished Your Story   58
• *More brainstorming?* • *Sequels* • *A famous example*

Glossary/Find out more/Index   60

WANT TO BE A WRITER?

This book aims to give you the tools to write your own science fiction. Learn how to craft believable characters, perfect plots, and satisfying beginnings, middles and endings.

Step-by-step instruction

The pages throughout the book include numbers providing step-by-step instructions or a series of options that will help you to master certain parts of the writing process. To create beginnings, middles and ends, for example, complete 18 simple steps.

Chronological progress

You can follow your progress by using the bar located on the bottom of each page. The orange colour tells you how far along the story-writing process you have got. As the blocks are filled out, so your story will be gathering pace...

28 THE SUPPORTING CAST

❻ The rest of the cast

In science fiction as in real life, y heroes and villains will be judged by the company they keep. Scene between them and minor charac are a good way to show readers w your main characters are really li

You can show them being mean or brave in scenes with someone else.

❼ Creating characters

Minor characters won't be as developed as heroes and villains, but they must seem 'real'. Base them on someone you know or find some striking characteristic that brings them to life. For example, Marvin the android (left) in Douglas Adams' *The Hitchhiker's Guide to the Galaxy* is always whingeing about being depressed. C-3PO in *Star Wars* may be clever but he complains a lot too and often isn't very brave. And when the little alien Beebo is around in Bruce Coville's *Alien Classmate* series you always know that he is going to cause chaos.

TIPS AND TECHNIQUES

The supporters of your hero or villain – whether spaceship crew or aliens – must help to move your story forward. If they haven't a job to do, cut them out. Showing not telling is the key to exciting story-telling.

GETTING STARTED | WRITING STYLES AND IDEAS | CREATING CHARACTERS | VI

Each section explains a key part of the writing process, teaching you how to get into the mindset of an author and learn all the necessary skills, from plot structure and viewpoints to adding belieavable dialogue. The process ends by looking at the next step – what do you want to do next after your story is finished.

Box features

Appearing throughout the book, these four different colour-coded box types help you with the writing process by providing inspiration, examples from other books, background details and hints and tips.

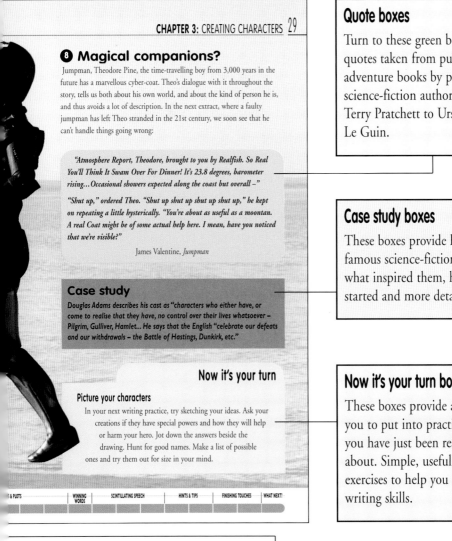

CHAPTER 3: CREATING CHARACTERS 29

❽ Magical companions?

Jumpman, Theodore Pine, the time-travelling boy from 3,000 years in the future has a marvellous cyber-coat. Theo's dialogue with it throughout the story, tells us both about his own world, and about the kind of person he is, and thus avoids a lot of description. In the next extract, where a faulty jumpman has left Theo stranded in the 21st century, we soon see that he can't handle things going wrong:

> *"Atmosphere Report, Theodore, brought to you by Realfish. So Real You'll Think It Swam Over For Dinner! It's 23.8 degrees, barometer rising…Occasional showers expected along the coast but overall –"*
>
> *"Shut up," ordered Theo. "Shut up shut up shut up shut up," he kept on repeating a little hysterically. "You're about as useful as a moontan. A real Coat might be of some actual help here. I mean, have you noticed that we're visible?"*
>
> James Valentine, *Jumpman*

Case study

Douglas Adams describes his cast as "characters who either have, or come to realise that they have, no control over their lives whatsoever – Pilgrim, Gulliver, Hamlet… He says that the English "celebrate our defeats and our withdrawals – the Battle of Hastings, Dunkirk, etc."

Now it's your turn

Picture your characters

In your next writing practice, try sketching your ideas. Ask your creations if they have special powers and how they will help or harm your hero. Jot down the answers beside the drawing. Hunt for good names. Make a list of possible ones and try them out for size in your mind.

& PLOTS | WINNING WORDS | SCINTILLATING SPEECH | HINTS & TIPS | FINISHING TOUCHES | WHAT NEXT!

Quote boxes

Turn to these green boxes to find quotes taken from published adventure books by popular science-fiction authors, from Terry Pratchett to Ursula K. Le Guin.

Case study boxes

These boxes provide history on famous science-fiction writers - what inspired them, how they started and more details.

Now it's your turn boxes

These boxes provide a chance for you to put into practice what you have just been reading about. Simple, useful and fun exercises to help you build your writing skills.

Tips and techniques boxes

These boxes provide writing tips that will help you when you get stuck, or provide added inspiration to get you to the next level.

WHY DO WRITERS WRITE?

You can learn a great deal from hearing how successful writers came to write. No writer would say that writing is easy. Most well-known writers will have toiled for years before seeing their first stories in print. They write to tell a story that must be told, and because they believe that nothing is more important than stories.

Terry Pratchett

Famous for his *Discworld* books, he published his first Sci-Fi story in his school magazine when he was thirteen. Two years later he was published professionally in the magazine Science Fantasy. He says this:

We're living in science fiction, but we don't realize it. I was buying something for my wife in Perth, Australia, last time I was on tour.
I couldn't remember her size, so I phoned her up…That is a science fiction conversation! All the more so for being mundane. I'm actually making a phone call all around the world on my mobile phone, to ask my wife her dress size!

L. Frank Baum

Not a Sci-Fi writer – he wrote the *Wizard of Oz* – but what he had to say about writing is especially true of science fiction:

Imagination has given us the steam engine, the telephone, the talking machine, and the automobile, for these things had to be dreamed of before they became realities. So I believe that dreams – day dreams…with your eyes wide open…are likely to leadto the betterment of the world.

Ursula K. Le Guin

She advises young writers to care about what words mean and how they use them. She wrote her first time-travel story when she was ten years old, but when she failed to publish it, she stopped writing and spent the next nine years reading. She says that:

Science fiction begins at the moment where science ends, and then you go on and build on what is known.

Read and read the best. One doesn't have to have scientific knowledge…If I need to know anything for my story, I go to the library and read about it.
I think most science-fiction writers work this way.

TIPS AND TECHNIQUES

Science fiction can sometimes become science fact. Both forms of invention begin in the human imagination.

FIRST THINGS FIRST

While real-life scientists need hi-tech laboratories and expensive research programmes to conduct their experiments, science-fiction writers only need a pen, paper and their imagination. They need a good library too, or access to the internet to explore the latest scientific ideas that might inspire new stories.

❶ Gather your writing materials

As you follow the advice in this book, you may find that some of the following will help you to organize your creative efforts:

- A small notebook that you carry everywhere
- Pencils and pens with alien-coloured ink
- Different coloured post-it notes to mark any ideas during your research
- Stick-on stars to highlight your best ideas

- Folders for all your bits of useful research and to keep your brainstorming exercises to refer to later
- A dictionary
- A thesaurus
- An encyclopaedia
- A computer or word processor

❷ Find a writing place

You will need a special writing place. Writers are lucky. They can work where they choose. Roald Dahl turned his garden shed into his special creative zone. You could make your bedroom your centre of operations, or perhaps your local internet café or library has just the right atmosphere. Wherever you write, sit up straight while you are writing. Hunched up work blocks the flow of oxygen to the brain, and that means foggy thinking.

❸ Create a writing zone

- Play the right music to spark those story ideas

- Put up a poster showing Planet Earth from space or a selection of hi-tech images that especially intrigue you

- Put on a hat or scarf that you only wear when you're writing

- Gather around you some mysterious objects to inspire your spirit of enquiry – a rock crystal or a fossil that you found (evidence of some alien life-form?)

Spend time choosing these things. Your writing place is important – special things are going to happen there.

TIPS AND TECHNIQUES

Once you have found your writing place, the golden rule of becoming a real writer is: Go there as often as possible, and write something! This is calle the writer's golden rule.

❹ Get in training

Before astronauts head for the stars, they must undergo long training programmes to prepare them for conditions in space. Becoming a writer is very like this. Don't just write when you feel like it. If all writers did this there would be far fewer books on the planet.

Now it's your turn

Learn to unlock your imagination

Try this brainstorming exercise. Have pens and scrap paper ready, plus a timer. Then sit quietly in your writing zone for a few moments. Set the timer for two minutes and write the phrase 'space-time continuum' at the top of the paper. Now, without taking the pen from the page, you are going to write all the science-fiction words, phrases and names you first think of. Don't worry about spelling or if it's rubbish. SPLURGE like a meteor shower! Then stop when two minutes are up. Brilliant! You've proved you can write.

MARTIAN
SPACEMAN
KRYPTONITE
METEOR
ALIEN

➎ Reward yourself!

When you've finished the task above, give yourself a gold star. You are on your way to the finding the *Lost Mines of Your Imagination.* The more you do exercises like this, the easier it will be to overcome the writer's worst enemy – the Story Spectre. The voice in your head that continually picks fault with your writing, also called your internal critic.

TIPS AND TECHNIQUES

Keep all your brainstorming notes in a file or notebook. You will need them later. Don't let a Martian invasion or approaching asteroids stop your writing practise. Fix a time slot and stick to it.

Case study

When Sci-Fi writer Robert J. Sawyer was in high school he started a Sci-Fi addicts club. With fellow members, he wrote scripts for a radio drama series that was never made. Later, Sawyer cut out all ideas that hadn't been his and shaped his first saleable story called **Motive***. Many of the ideas in this first story – a murderous computer and dinosaur-like aliens were developed in his later novels, including his first novel* **The Golden Fleece***.*

❻ Read, read, read!

Before you can write science fiction you need
to know what it is. In libraries and bookstores
you will usually find Sci-Fi and fantasy books
side by side. Both these genres (story types) are
called 'speculative fiction' because they are set
in imagined worlds that could not exist.

❼ Discover the meaning of Sci-Fi

Fantasy worlds are usually governed by magic. The stories have forces of
good and evil trying to find ways to increase or overcome each
other's power. The storytellers must say what their own magic
rules are before they develop their tale too far. In science fiction,
the speculative worlds also have rules, but they are based on
known scientific principles that have been imagined to
another stage of development. For example, the main rule
in time-travel stories is that the traveller should not change
anything in the time zones they visit.

❽ Read widely

Reading other writers' work will help develop your own special
interests and make it easier for you to discover what you really
want to write about. Try to read different types of science
fiction. Start with some of the classic writers – H. G.
Wells, Jules Verne, John Wyndham, Isaac Asimov,
Arthur C. Clarke, Ursula K. Le Guin. As you read
them, look for the kinds of story ideas that excite
you most.

TIPS AND TECHNIQUES

*When thinking up your own stories – watch out for clichés.
A cliché is an idea that has been used too many times before.
Like Cling-on Attacks, they are best avoided.*

❾ Choose a theme

These are the main themes used by Sci-Fi authors in a selection of their books.

- Alien invasions – H. G. Wells' *The War of the Worlds*
- Robots and androids – Isaac Asimov's *Robot* series
- Time travel – H. G. Wells' *The Time Machine*
- Monsters out of place and time – Jules Verne's *Journey to the Centre of the Earth*
- Virtual Reality gone too far – Alan Gibbons' *Shadow of the Minotaur*
- Life on other planets – Ursula K. Le Guin's *The Left Hand of Darkness*
- Civilizations under threat – Octavia Butler, *Xenogenesis* series
- Space exploration – *Star Trek* series
- Space wars – Orson Scott Card's *Ender's Game*; *Star Wars* series
- Our future world – M. T. Anderson's *Feed*; Neil Arksey's *Playing on the Edge*
- Humorous science fiction – Douglas Adams' *The Hitchhiker's Guide to the Galaxy*; Terry Pratchett's *Discworld* series

❿ Take notes

As you read, keep a science-fiction log. Note down what books you have read, briefly say what they were about and why you enjoyed them. Make notes, do drawings. Start a character collection. You will need them later.

Now it's your turn

Operation brainstorm

Think 'Outer Space'. In a two-minute timed practice, jot down as many different words you can think of to describe it – empty, void, black, airless? Does it have sounds and smells? What would they be?

A WRITER'S VOICE

The more you read, the more you will learn about writing, but you must have your writer's scanner switched on first. As you read, ask questions: how does the writer make their story's world and characters so convincing? How did they build suspense or make the story's ending so satisfying?

❶ Finding your voice

Once you start reading as a writer you will notice that each story has its own rhythm and range of language that stays the same throughout the book. You will get to know different writers' styles. H. G. Wells is worlds apart from Douglas Adams, Orson Scott Card writes very differently from Ursula K. Le Guin. In other words, you will discover their distinctive VOICE, one that you can often recognize in much the same way that you know your favourite rock band when you hear their new song on the radio.

Case study

Alan Gibbons, author of **The Shadow of the Minotaur,** *got the writing bug from reading and reading. He says "I don't see how you can be a good writer without being a good reader."*

❷ Experiment

Once you've found an author whose books you really enjoy, it's tempting to stick to them. Don't! Experiment. Once in a while read something quite different: a historical novel or a book of legends. You may be surprised what ideas it gives you.

WRITERS' VOICES

Look at the kinds of words these writers use. Do they use many adjectives or long sentences? Are they convincing? Which style do you prefer to read?

ARTHUR C. CLARKE

It was the last days of the Empire. The tiny ship was far from home, and almost a hundred light-years from the great parent vessel searching through the loosely packed stars at the rim of the Milky Way. But even here it could not escape from the shadow that lay across civilization.

Arthur C. Clarke, *Encounter at Dawn*

PHILIP REEVE

Hester Shaw was starting to get used to being happy. After all her muddy, starveling years in the ditches and scavenger-villes of the Great Hunting Ground she had finally found herself a place in the world. She had her own airship, the Jenny Haniver . . .

Philip Reeve, *Predator's Gold*

DOUGLAS ADAMS

. . . Zaphod Beeblebrox, President of the Imperial Intergalactic Government, sped across the seas of Damogran, his ion drive delta boat winking and flashing in the Damogran sun.

Douglas Adams, *The Hitchhiker's Guide to the Galaxy*

JAMES VALENTINE

Again, Jules was amazed at Gen's ability to keep up with all this. He was still being distracted by Theodore's hair, which was now a broad stripe of yellow with red and green lightning bolts flashing on either side, and whenever the time travel stuff came up he could feel the entire concept slipping away from him, like most of what his maths teacher said.

James Valentine, *Jumpman*

H. G. WELLS

The living intelligence, the Martian within the hood, was slain and splashed to the four windows of heaven, and the thing was now a mere intricate device of metal whirling to its destruction.

H.G. Wells, *The War of the Worlds*

❸ Idea search

Science-fiction writers usually explore big ideas in their stories – the end of civilization as we know it, for example. The imagined crises they describe challenge us to think about our lives now, and wonder how things might be in the future. Writers are continually absorbing information about subjects that interest them. Their data-gathering scanners are always on full alert, whether they are watching TV or chatting with friends, or even when they are asleep. They make notes and read everything that might spark an idea or develop their knowledge.

❹ Don't panic!

If you are stuck for story ideas, don't panic! That will just make your brain go blank. In fact, you already have lots of ideas, locked away in deep inside your imagination. This is where your subconscious memory stores every story experience you ever had. If you can try and relax, and don't pressure yourself, these stories will begin to find their way out of your head and onto the page.

TIPS AND TECHNIQUES

Brainstorm when you are bored or nervous – in your dentist's waiting room or while waiting to take a test. You may come up with your best ideas, and it takes your mind off everything. Make lists. How many ways can you describe yellow? How many metals can you think of? How dark is dark? How far is far? Tap the Hidden Depths of Your Imagination.

❺ Freeing your stories

Your subconscious mind is probably already full of story ideas
–the books you've read, the films you've watched, all those
episodes of the X-files. It is only in your conscious mind that you
forget these things. To write your own stories you need to
access and recycle all that creative stuff in your
subconscious mind. Brainstorming and
asking 'What If' questions are good
ways to start.

Case study

It was a simple newspaper headline 'Language is a virus' that made Sci-Fi writer Lisa Tuttle start wondering: What if human speech was indeed caused by an ancient virus embedded in our DNA, and what if we accidentally 'cured' ourselves of it, in our obsession to eradicate diseases? From these questions grew her story **The Cure.**

Now it's your turn

Brainstorming

Today, you discovered you were an
android, the only one in your family?
Ask yourself these questions: How did I
discover it? How does it make me feel?
Does it explain why I often feel different from
everyone else, and if so in what ways? Do I have some
special talent that makes my schoolmates jealous? Now write
for 20 minutes. If you think you have the makings of a good story,
develop it.

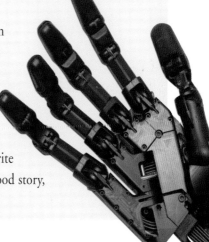

❻ Get researching

Having a story idea is just the start. Next comes much research while you develop the idea into a story. You will need some science facts and some real-world information to grow a good story. Start the gathering process. Note down any good ideas or interesting information in your notebook. Maybe you can use your own interests or special knowledge – of computer games, sport, astronomy – to develop some future scenario. Making your story scientifically accurate is a great way to grab your reader's attention and bring them into your world.

❼ Where to look

• Search for related articles in the popular press.

• Look out for doom and gloom headlines.

• Look for direct quotes. What awful or extraordinary things have happened to people. Their words might trigger your own characters.

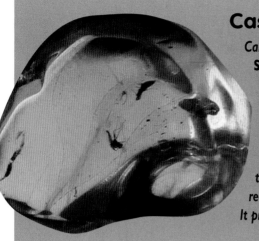

Case study

Canadian Sci-Fi writer Robert J. Sawyer uses **Science News** *for his science facts. It was here that he read about prehistoric mosquitoes trapped in amber and the possibility of dinosaur blood being preserved in their bellies: Could it be used to clone dinosaurs? the article posed. 'Neat!' he thought and turned the page. When writer Michael Crichton read the same article, he thought 'Ye-ees!' It prompted him to write* **Jurassic Park**.

- Search for more specialist articles in the national press or on media websites. CNN and BBC News have good popular science coverage.

- Read popular science journals:
  Science News, New Scientist, National Geographic, Astronomy etc.

TIPS AND TECHNIQUES

Start a dream diary to tap into your subconscious mind. Have a notebook beside your bed and write down any dream ideas as soon as you wake up.

Now it's your turn

BUILDING WORLDS

Once your story ideas start simmering, you can help things along by building the physical world where your story will take place. Repeat the exercise on page 11. See if it's taken more shape? Can you feel your ideas developing? Do you need some more…?

❽ Discovering a setting

The setting or speculative world in a Sci-Fi story is as important as the story itself. On his writing website, Robert J. Sawyer says, 'One of the key skills for a Sci-Fi writer is world building – creating a convincing alternate reality...'

❾ Laying down the law

Earlier in the chapter you looked at ways to develop your story idea by doing research. World building requires a similar process. The 'scientific laws' that rule your world must work for your readers, so first ask yourself these questions:

- What are the rules in my world? Does it have night and day, seasons, different limates? Is it natural or man-made? Is it Earth in the past or future?

- What are its colours, smells, textures?

- And what big disaster is looming – the loss of vital resources, an epidemic, a war?

- Who will suffer most and whose story is most important?

Case study

You don't always need an extraordinary setting for good science fiction. In **Dinosaur Summer**, Greg Bear sets the story in 1947, as a sequel to Arthur Conan Doyle's **The Lost World**. This was the first Sci-Fi dinosaur story, published in 1912, and in it Doyle's character Professor Challenger discovers a population of surviving dinosaurs on a South American jungle plateau. Greg Bear picks up the tale thirty-five years on. It is a good example of a writer building on an existing story without copying it.

Now it's your turn

Brainstorming: It's a wonderful world

Think about another world you would really like to visit. Imagine it's your job to attract new colonists to your Sci-Fi world. In ten minutes brainstorm some sales blurb to sell its attractions.

Next, write a different view in a diary account. This time, reveal your secret doubts about encouraging new settlers. There are signs that things in your world aren't so good, but why then are your world's rulers so keen to attract newcomers? Take ten minutes. Don't think too hard – write top-of-your-head thoughts.

⑩ Building a world

World building is like writing a geography assignment and creating the geography too. But you can use magazines, books and computer games to imagine it better. Create a profile of your world. Draw maps and plans. Think yourself into it:

- What is there?
- How do people live and travel around?
- What are their houses like?
- What do people wear, eat?
- Are there aliens, robots, thinking computers?

TIPS AND TECHNIQUES

In a good Sci-Fi story, your characters' world will always be under some major threat. Check out 'Science and Space' on www.CNN.com. The headlines could spark a tale. Here are two recent ones: 'Woman 'tastes' musical notes' and 'Hidden galaxies spotted'.

⑪ Don't go over the top!

New writers find world building very absorbing. Some try to invent a new language with extraordinary names for everything they have created. This makes life too hard for readers. Instead, focus on how your world works, and how its amazing aspects will affect your characters and their story.

⑫ Make your setting real

To make your setting real for readers you need to trigger their senses. You can do this with:

• Straight description. Tell the reader what it's like.

• Through your characters' direct experience. Show the reader what it is like.

• Use analogy. Compare your world to somewhere your readers do know.

Most people have never been in zero gravity, but Orson Scott Card finds a common human experience to describe his battleroom:

> *They filed clumsily into the battleroom, like children in a swimming pool for the first time, clinging to the handholds along the side. They soon found that things went better if they didn't use their feet at all.*
>
> Orson Scott Card, *Ender's Game*

⓭ Define the threat

Whatever is threatening your world, it will affect the way you describe your setting. Look again at the opening of the Arthur C. Clarke story on page 15. See how it tells you where you are and combines action (travelling through space) with an instant sense of foreboding: 'the shadow that lay across civilization'.

Now your Sci-Fi world should be taking shape, and you have a good crisis lurking, so it's time to find out who your characters are…

TIPS AND TECHNIQUES

A key storytelling skill is to say just enough to move the story forward, while hinting that there is much more still to find out. If your world needs a lot of explaining, try putting the main details in a prologue. Write it from the perspective of one of your characters.

Now it's your turn

A dramatic opening

Write an opening story scene of about 200 words. Take ten minutes. Combine setting details with some piece of action – maybe your hero arriving. Try adding a hint of doom too. Choose the most descriptive verbs you can think of. For example, a starship doesn't just fly, it speeds through space; a power-plant throbs with pent-up energy; a red sun looms through the solar dust.

HEROES

Your hero or heroes (protagonists) are the lead actors in your story. You must care about them deeply and make readers feel the same way. Think of them as new friends. Sometimes they will surprise you.

❶ Finding a hero

Sci-Fi films and books have marvellous heroes to inspire you. You can use them as role models and mix them with people you know. Will yours be like brave Princess Leia in *Star Wars*? Or what about the boy, David, in Steven Spielberg's film *A.I.*, who looks human but is really a humanoid robot and longs to be a real boy. Ender in Ender's Game, is a six-year-old child prodigy who is being trained as a battle commander for a future space war.

Now it's your turn

Know your hero

If your hero hasn't yet taken shape, here's a way to help.

On a large sheet of paper roughly map out a square of 36 boxes, six across the top, six down the side. Write these headings in the boxes down the side:

1) physical appearance 2) clothing 3) behaviour 4) strengths 5) failings 6) favourite things. Now brainstorm for five minutes. Filling in the squares across the page, write down the first things you think of about your hero's looks. Do the same for the other categories. When you have finished you will know thirty things about your hero. Some might be weird. Some you might discard. Some might trigger a whole new set of ideas.

➋ Choose the right name

Discovering your hero's name can sometimes bring them to life at once. Ask them what they are called. If you're stuck, try the names' list in baby books or on the internet, or flick through an atlas index or telephone book. If you make a name up, say it out loud first; see what it sounds like. Don't make it too complicated for readers to read. Leia, R2-D2, David, Lina, Doon are simple but pleasing. They have a poetic ring.

LEIA   R2-D2   DOON   LINA

➌ Give strengths and weaknesses

No one wants to read stories about people with perfect lives. Heroes need serious personal problems as well as some major external threat to overcome. In Loise Lawrence's *Dreamweaver*, Eth's major personal problem revolves round her cruel brother Liadd, but this story also weaves into a wider threat: her planet is about to be colonized by greedy Earth settlers. Her strengths and weaknesses are played out between these two predicaments, adding drama and suspense.

TIPS AND TECHNIQUES

Start a 'special words' list in your notebook. Write down any word that catches your imagination. You'll know where to look the next time you are stuck for a name. Use your own experiences and emotions to help you build your characters. Think how you felt when something bad happened to you.

❹ What type of villain?

In science fiction your hero's main external enemy is likely to be some physical disaster, but you also need some enemy characters too. They might be absolutely evil like Darth Vader, or their wickedness might not be so easy to spot.

❺ The face of evil

First think about what makes your villains so evil. Are they hungry for power? Do they want great wealth or some special knowledge that will help them control everyone, or make them immortal? Are they simply cruel and get their pleasure from destroying things? Are they envious of your hero? Did they start off good and then turn to evil ways?

Now it's your turn

Know your villain

In a ten-minute practice, brainstorm your chief villain. What is his motivation? Think about his or her weaknesses too and how these might help the story. Repeat the exercise on page 24 with your baddy as your focus.

TIPS AND TECHNIQUES

The more you question your villains, the more you'll find out about them, and the more intriguing they'll become. Sometimes the most evil thing is something you can't quite see. The writer can reveal it indirectly through the fear in the characters' minds.

Villainous Profiles
Here are some ideas for different types of baddies:

HUMAN EVIL

In Louise Lawrence's Dreamweaver, *Eth tries to make her brother Liadd less cruel by weaving him better dreams as he sleeps, but his psychic self wakes and attacks her.*

UNIVERSE DOMINATION

The most frightening thing about George Lucas' evil creation, Darth Vader is that he was once an ordinary man. But with his cyborg implants and deadly pursuit of evil power, he has turned into a blood-chilling man-machine.

MONSTROUS PURSUERS

Greg Bear's main predator is the huge Death Eagle, who stalk the pages of Dinosaur Summer. *With its 'scimitar beak', 'knife-like teeth' and 'black-feathered arms', it stops the readers' hearts whenever they hear its terrible cries across the jungle plateau.*

LURKING THREAT

Orson Scott Card hardly lets us see the bug-like invaders in Ender's Game. *We fear them because Ender himself is so desperate to save his sister, so they 'won't split her skull with a beam so hot that her brains burst the skull'.*

ALIENS ON EARTH

In The Day of the Triffids, *John Wyndham's aliens are ten-foot-high walking plants that attack humanity.*

CYBER EVIL

In Arthur C. Clarke's 2001: A Space Odyssey, *the thinking, feeling computer HAL 9000 receives conflicting human messages and develops murderous inclinations towards its spaceship's human crew.*

❻ The rest of the cast

In science fiction as in real life, your heroes and villains will be judged by the company they keep. Scenes between them and minor characters are a good way to show readers what your main characters are really like. You can show them being mean or brave in scenes with someone else.

❼ Creating characters

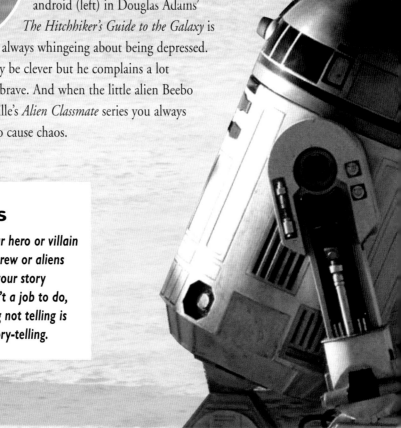

Minor characters won't be as developed as heroes and villains, but they must seem 'real'. Base them on someone you know or find some striking characteristic that brings them to life. For example, Marvin the android (left) in Douglas Adams' *The Hitchhiker's Guide to the Galaxy* is always whingeing about being depressed. C-3PO in *Star Wars* may be clever but he complains a lot too and often isn't very brave. And when the little alien Beebo is around in Bruce Coville's *Alien Classmate* series you always know that he is going to cause chaos.

TIPS AND TECHNIQUES

The supporters of your hero or villain – whether spaceship crew or aliens – must help to move your story forward. If they haven't a job to do, cut them out. Showing not telling is the key to exciting story-telling.

⑧ Magical companions?

Jumpman, Theodore Pine, the time-travelling boy from 3,000 years in the future has a marvellous cyber-coat. Theo's dialogue with it throughout the story, tells us both about his own world, and about the kind of person he is, and thus avoids a lot of description. In the next extract, where a faulty jumpman has left Theo stranded in the 21st century, we soon see that he can't handle things going wrong:

> *"Atmosphere Report, Theodore, brought to you by Realfish. So Real You'll Think It Swam Over For Dinner! It's 23.8 degrees, barometer rising…Occasional showers expected along the coast but overall –"*
>
> *"Shut up," ordered Theo. "Shut up shut up shut up shut up," he kept on repeating a little hysterically. "You're about as useful as a moontan. A real Coat might be of some actual help here. I mean, have you noticed that we're visible?"*
>
> James Valentine, *Jumpman*

Case study

Douglas Adams describes his cast as "characters who either have, or come to realise that they have, no control over their lives whatsoever – Pilgrim, Gulliver, Hamlet… He says that the English "celebrate our defeats and our withdrawals – the Battle of Hastings, Dunkirk, etc."

Now it's your turn

Picture your characters

In your next writing practice, try sketching your ideas. Ask your creations if they have special powers and how they will help or harm your hero. Jot down the answers beside the drawing. Hunt for good names. Make a list of possible ones and try them out for size in your mind.

WHO'S SPEAKING?

You have a story to tell, but before you can start, you must decide on your story's 'point of view'. Do you want to tell the readers everything that is happening and show all the characters' views? Or do you want to tell one particular person's story? You have several options...

❶ An all-seeing view

The omniscient or all-seeing view is a way of writing that means that the narrator sits outside the events that are going on around him, and can describe how any of the characters in his or her story are feeling at any time. This way of writing is not common in science fiction.

❷ The third-person view

Science Fiction is more often told from the point of view (POV) of the main character. This is called third person viewpoint. This is usually written in the past tense. When writing from this limited viewpoint, you cannot suddenly switch and say what the humans thought of Galt – not unless Galt actually knows their opinion. In which case he might say something like:

> *Counsellor Galt bowed briefly, and turned on his heel. He must not show his anger to these inferior beings. Humans! Let the universe be rid of their selfish, muddle-headed thinking.*
>
> Tish Farrell

❸ The multiple viewpoint

Short stories are usually written from one viewpoint, two at most. But in novels there can be multiple viewpoints. This adds to the story's suspense and complexity. The *Animorphs* series, by K.A. Applegate, has five alternating viewpoints, each chapter switching to one of the five main characters. It is fast-paced and plot-driven – what is happening is more important than developing the characters. All the characters speak in the first person, which is an exciting point of view to use.

Now it's your turn

Write a scene

Take half an hour to write a short scene from your own story. Describe your hero battling with some villain. First write from the all-knowing viewpoint, describing what is happening on both sides as they fight. Then re-write it in the third person past tense, giving only your hero's viewpoint. Finally, write in the first person as if you are the hero.

TIPS AND TECHNIQUES

The first-person viewpoint can make an extraordinary tale sound true. You could write your story as a starship log or a series of letters. You might be a human survivor of some disaster or a mad scientist documenting your experiments!

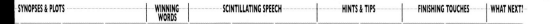

READY TO WRITE

When your story starts bubbling fiercely in your mind, it's a good idea to write a few paragraphs about it. This brief account is called a synopsis and will help you keep your story on track. Tell just enough to be intriguing but **DON'T GIVE AWAY THE END!**

❶ Back cover inspiration

To get some ideas, look at the back covers of some Sci-Fi books and read the blurb. See how they say just enough to whet your appetite: you simply have to findout what happens next.

The synopsis for *Playing on the Edge*, by Neil Arksey, imagines a scenario where the world's leading sportsmen and women achieve victory thanks in part to a cocktail of performance enhancing drugs:

> *On Easy Linker's thirteenth birthday, in 2064, he's bought by Gunman Reds, one of the UK super-teams. Now he'll be pumped full of performance-enhancers so that he'll be a star player at fourteen... no one inside or outside the game questions what they are doing... But Easy manages to escape with evidence that will destroy them – all he has to do is stay free for long enough...*
>
> Neil Arksey, *Playing on the Edge*

Now it's your turn

Write your blurb

Sum up your story in a single striking sentence, then develop it in two or three short paragraphs. Think about your potential readers and try to draw them in to make them want to read the book.

❷ Create a synopsis

Novelists often list all their chapters before they start writing, and say briefly what will happen in each one. This is called a chapter synopsis. It stops them losing track of the story once they start writing.

❸ Make a story map

You have a synopsis that says what your story is about. You have a cast of characters and a setting, and you know from whose viewpoint you wish to tell the tale. The last thing you need before you tell your tale is a story map.

❹ Split into scenes

Before film-makers can start filming, they must know the main story episodes and decide how they can best tell their story in filmed images. To help them, they make a story map by outlining the plot (the sequence of events) in a series of sketches called storyboards. You can do this for your story. Draw the main episodes in pictures. Add a few notes that say what is happening in each scene.

TIPS AND TECHNIQUES

If you can't sum up your story as simply as the extract on page 32, it is possibly too complicated, so simplify it. As you work on your own synopsis, start asking yourself 'Whose story is this and how will I tell it?'

❺ Think about your theme

At the same time as thinking about your scenes, give some thought to your story's theme. In science fiction this might be the end of civilization as we know it; or the rights and wrongs of exploiting another life form; or what it means to be human; or what it would be like for an alien life form on Earth, as is the case with the Superman stories.

❻ Get inspiration from a classic

Here are some possible storyboard captions for *Gulliver's Adventures in Lilliput*, written by Jonathan Swift and published in 1726. The story is widely regarded to be the first piece of science fiction written.

1. Gulliver shipwrecked and washed ashore;
2. Wakes up to find himself captured by Lilliputians;
3. Meets the Emperor and six Lilliputians shoot at him;
4. Gulliver's kindness to his attackers earns Emperor's favour;
5. Reviews the troops and learns of war with Blefuscu;
6. Gulliver saves Lilliput by dragging enemy ships to Lilliput;
7. Refuses to destroy the enemy and is charged with treason;
8. Lilliputian courtiers plot against Gulliver urging his death;
9. Emperor lessens punishment to blinding, but Gulliver flees
10. Gulliver finds a boat, escapes to sea where he is rescued.

❼ Decide to write a novel?

Novels aren't short stories made longer, but short stories made fatter. They still have beginnings, middles and ends, and heroes with problems and conflicts, but the main story is expanded with subplots and

Now it's your turn

Weave a story web

In the middle of a large piece of paper, draw a rough sketch of your hero within a circle. As you are drawing, imagine that you are that hero, trying to decide which way to go. Think about the problems you have and what you are going to do about them. Draw six spokes round your hero circle. Each leads to another circle. Inside each one sketch a different scene, or write it as notes. Each circle will be some new course of action that you might take, or some obstacle that an enemy sets in your path. Give yourself 20 minutes.

many more characters and incidents. Novels are usually divided into chapters which also have beginnings, middles and ends. Once you have worked out the main episodes or scenes in your story, you can decide if you are going to tell them simply and briefly as a short story, or develop each one further as a chapter for a novel.

❽ Or a short story...

To turn *Gulliver's Adventures in Lilliput* into a short story, the original novel's chapters are reduced to a few key scenes like the captions. These are then retold more briefly. *Gulliver's Adventures in Lilliput* works well as a shorter story. It has a hero with problems, some conflict in the middle, a climax and a hopeful ending. The book also has a good theme about the use and abuse of power.

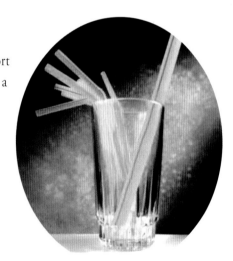

TIPS AND TECHNIQUES

Don't let a novel's length put you off from starting one. If you use the story map approach it is often easier to write a novel than it is to write a good short story.

❾ Dramatic beginnings

You have planned your plot and are ready to start telling your own story. It is time for blast off. Focus on your hero. How will you win the readers to their cause? A good beginning is critical.

❿ A starting point

Many stories start at the point when their heroes' lives are 'normal'. They may have their usual problems, but nothing much is happening. Then comes some crisis or external conflict that turns their lives upside down. Something has to be done about it. The advantage of doing this, is that the readers can share the hero's shock when the crisis happens. Other stories leap straight into some powerful action, and this is so involving that the readers are instantly hooked. Only then will the writers pause to give some of the characters' backstory or history, which will explain the opening scene.

TIPS AND TECHNIQUES

Story beginnings introduce the hero, reveal their problems and start the quest to resolve them. Use your library to study opening sentences. Write down your favourites. Work on your own beginning sentence. Write it and re-write it. Read it aloud.

Your opening sentence

Once you have thought up a good opening scene that makes your hero seem really interesting, you must work out a mind-grabbing first sentence. Here are some good ways:

Create mystery

> *Inside the hangar it was as dark as razor-rat's hole. At one end, a crack in the panels let in a single bright shaft of light. It looked like an escape route from hell.*
>
> Sue Welford, *Flight for Freedom*

Make your character sympathetic

> *"Michela Corbin, what did I just say?" The class began to snigger. I looked up dismayed ...but the teacher was too quick for me. She snatched up the screen and started to read the story I'd been writing. I groaned. I was in deep, deep trouble. Again!*
>
> Malorie Blackman, *Peacemaker*

Stir strong emotions and be mysterious

> *"Mother!?"*
> *There was no reply. She hadn't expected one. Her mother had been dead now for four days, and Kira could tell that the last of the spirit was drifting away.*
>
> Lois Lowry, *Gathering Blue*

Be dramatic or funny

> *John Watt eyed the Big Red Button nervously. "What does it do?" he asked. Vernon Bright raised a mysterious finger. "Aha," he said. John gave Bright a worried look. It wasn't exactly that he didn't trust him. Bright was very reliable – unfortunately. He could be relied on to cause chaos, mayhem and panic wherever he went...*
>
> Steve Barlow & Steve Skidmore, *Vernon Bright and the Faster Than Light Show*

⓫ False happy endings

If story beginnings must grip, then middles should grip harder. From the first page the story needs to build tension and suspense. If your story is drifting then try to see things through your characters' eyes. One good ploy to create suspense is to have a false happy ending.

For example, the hero seems to have saved the world from invasion, but just when everyone is celebrating, a more deadly alien force appears on the planet's scanners. This gives the writer the chance to build up the excitement on an even bigger scale.

⓬ Maintain the action

Plenty of activity also holds readers' interest. Keep your characters engaged with their quest at all times, on the move, working things out, coming to the wrong conclusions, having fights, escaping disasters.

⓭ Give your heroes problems

If your heroes are time-challenged this instantly adds drama. Will Ender be trained in time to destroy the next alien fleet (*Ender's Game*)? Will Eth learn what she must before the unwanted spacecraft lands on her planet (*Dreamweaver*)? Will Lina and Doon solve the problems of their dying city before the lights go out forever (*The City of Ember*)?

Now it's your turn

There's strength in weakness

Focus on your hero's flaws or weaknesses. In five minutes write your first thoughts on how these might complicate and add drama to your story. Do the same for any other main characters. Perhaps your hero's friend turns out to have doubtful motives. Think how these factors might bring your story to a climax.

Try the whole exercise again, but write with your non-writing hand. See what crops up…

14 Challenge your reader

Don't forget to stir and complicate and pile on the challenges. If your hero has been pursued by some bully or aggressor, make the reader think they have found a new target… then let the villain return with some worse torment. This time your hero must deal with this situation once and for all. How they decide to do this, and whether it will work, adds some new suspense. Your hero's weaknesses could come to the fore too.

TIPS AND TECHNIQUES

Action scenes should spring from the characters' own plans, not from your need to revive a flagging story. But when you do include them, make them as exciting as possible. Your characters' weaknesses can add more twists and turns to the story.

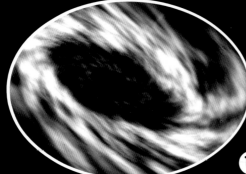

⓯ Choose an ending

Finding a good ending is perhaps the hardest part of storytelling. Some writers like to think up their exact ending before they start writing. Others don't want to know until they get there.

⓰ Wrapping up endings

As you plan your ending, think again about Problems, Conflict, and Resolution. Good endings must bring the hero's problems and conflicts (plot) to a climax, and then resolve them in satisfying ways. The ending should also refer in some way to the story's beginning and thus remind readers that something important has changed in the course of the story, e.g. the hero has overcome some weakness.

⓱ Create an intriguing finish

Most readers like some sort of happy ending, but dont be predictable. In science fiction the endings may have mixed feelings. Your heroes might have overcome some enemy and learned or gained something, but they may also have lost something, or had to make some sacrifices. So rather than a 'happy' end, make it hopeful instead. In *Star Wars*, when Luke Skywalker refuses to be lured to the dark side, Emperor Palpatine turns all his evil against him. Seeing his son being destroyed, Darth Vader destroys Palpatine but is wounded himself. Before he dies he asks Luke to remove the mask. He dies as Anakin Skywalker and not the monster he had become. For Luke this ending is desperately hard, gaining and losing his father all at once, but the forces of good have been saved.

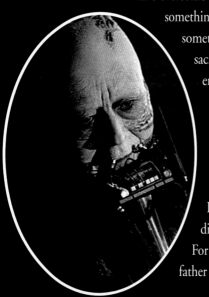

Now it's your turn

Choose your own ending

Read the ending of your favourite Sci-Fi story. Can you think of an alternative ending? See if you can write it, then put it aside. Go back and read both versions later. Now which ending do you prefer and why?

⑱ Add a twist

Many Sci-Fi stories have twist-in-the-tale endings. All along you've been assuming the enemy is an alien, but then you find out the humans are more dangerous. Or maybe an android turns out to have more humanity than its heartless human creator. To do this successfully you need to drop subtle clues throughout your story. This is called foreshadowing. The reader will be surprised by the twist, but will then think, 'I should have realized!'

Bad endings are one's that:

• Fizzle out because you've run out of ideas;

• Rely on some coincidence or surprise twist that hasn't been mentioned in the story;

• Fail to show how the characters have changed in some way;

• Are too grim and depressing and leave the reader with no hope.

TIPS AND TECHNIQUES

Don't forget to look at your story map if you are stuck. Or brainstorm your hero in a circle again from page 35.

MAKING WORDS WORK

Words are valuable things. Every one you use should work the hardest it can for your story. Readers can access your thrilling story so much more powerfully if it is free from rambling sentences and too many adjectives.

❶ Use vivid imagery

If you can sum up scenes in images that trigger the senses, it is like adding special effects to your story. Try using metaphors and similes to bring your story to life. These are word pictures. A metaphor is when you call a man a mouse, meaning that he is scared; a simile is a comparison: as quiet as a mouse. Choose striking verbs too.

In the Greg Bear example, one-syllable verbs like 'dropped' and 'thrust' are good action words that echo the activity. The 'truckload of knives' is a stunning simile. It knocks the breath out of you. Orson Scott Card uses a metaphor to describe Ender's space battle tactics in *Ender's Game*, followed by a simile:

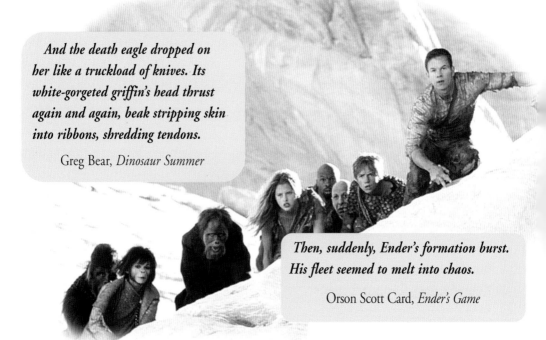

And the death eagle dropped on her like a truckload of knives. Its white-gorgeted griffin's head thrust again and again, beak stripping skin into ribbons, shredding tendons.

Greg Bear, *Dinosaur Summer*

Then, suddenly, Ender's formation burst. His fleet seemed to melt into chaos.

Orson Scott Card, *Ender's Game*

❷ Change the rhythm and length of your sentences

This is another way to keep readers reading. Like the Greg Bear example, action scenes need short, sharp phrases that focus exactly on what is happening. But if you are building up for something scary, spin out the phrases a little, add some sharp detail that make the scene more real. Imagine yourself creeping up on your reader…Then strike!

❸ Change the mood

Changes in mood will also give your story edge. Science fiction often deals with catastrophes, but if you are gloomy from start to finish, no one will want to read about it. In a tension-mounting scene some humour can give readers light relief. Or if your story is humorous, then try to give it some serious angles too. In the same way, readers also need a break from action sequences. This lets your readers catch their breath and allows the dust to settle before the story moves on.

Now it's your turn

Using words effectively

To make your writing bite, exercise your word-making skills. Brainstorm more lists: How many words for 'flying' can you think of? How many words for 'shine'? Reinvent sayings: the cliché 'As white as snow' could become 'As white as… a snow goose's tail, or a cannibal's smile, or an Alaskan snowdrift'. Read the dictionary. Play word games.

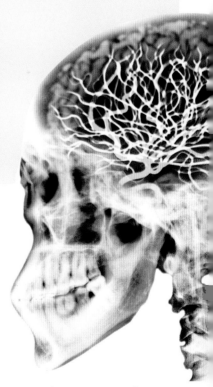

TIPS AND TECHNIQUES

Remember that your characters will have different moods too. Use them. Try ending a dramatic scene on a cliffhanger. Leave your heroes in peril and drive your readers to find out what happens next.

CREATING DIALOGUE

Dialogue lets readers hear your characters' own voices. Whether they are an alien or some human from the future, they must sound just right. Dialogue adds colour, pace, mood and suspense to your story.

❶ Let your characters speak for themselves

The best way to learn about dialogue is to switch on your listening ear and eavesdrop. Tune into the way people phrase their words. Write down any good idioms – someone saying 'sling yer hook' or 'shove off' instead of 'go away'. Watch people's body language too when they are whispering or arguing. Look, listen and absorb.

Now it's your turn

The art of writing good dialogue

Tune into a TV chat show, radio phone-in or observe conversations around you.. Spend ten minutes writing down what people say, including all the 'ums', 'ers' and repetition of their points. Listen out for a range of voices: young, old, different education or community. Next compare it with some dialogue in a book. You will see at once that written dialogue does not include all the hesitations of natural speech. These would be very tedious to read. Fictional dialogue, then, is a convention. It mimics real speech, but is not actually real.

❷ Following convention

The way dialogue is written down follows conventions or rules too. It is usual to start a new paragraph with every new speaker. What they say is enclosed in single or double inverted commas, followed by 'he said' or 'she said' to indicate the speaker. Notice that speech tags are left out in this exchange between Peter and his father when it is clear who is speaking. Simple speech verbs like 'said' and 'asked' are repeated and are not cluttered with adverbs such as loudly, quietly or angrily.

If you read the passage aloud you will find it has a good rhythmic flow that makes it easy to follow.

"I have a confession to make." Peter narrowed his eyes. "What sort of confession?" "I got a telegram from your mother. Last week. I didn't bother to tell you."

"Why?" Peter asked.
"It was addressed to me." Anthony returned to the front room and pulled the crumpled piece of paper from his shirt pocket. "She's worried about you. Summer's here. She thinks you're going to catch polio from all these crowds. She forbids you to swim in municipal pools." Peter had hoped his mother might have sent a message inviting him to come to Chicago for a visit . "Oh," he said.

Greg Bear, *Dinosaur Summer*

TIPS AND TECHNIQUES

When writing dialogue, don't just stick to 'he said/she said' all the time. Use words like 'asked', 'replied' 'exclaimed', 'cried', 'whispered', etc. to create excitement and variety in your writing.

❸ Why use dialogue?

Dialogue breaks up the blocks of narrative (storytelling), and gives readers' eyes a rest. It increases the pace because it is quicker to read and it's a direct way of giving readers information.

❹ Remember the viewpoint

If you are telling your story through one character's eyes, you can only give that character's opinions, thoughts and observations. They can't *know* what others are thinking and feeling (unless they are telepathic!). Dialogue lets readers hear other characters' views directly. Greg Bear's Peter/Anthony exchange on the previous page is written from Peter's viewpoint, for example. We watch Anthony through Peter's eyes and hear what he hears. We don't know what Anthony is thinking.

❺ Maintain momentum

Dialogue is a key way to move the story forward. Characters do not make idle chitchat. Whatever they say will convey information – about themselves, other characters and what is happening. You can use it to reveal their history, or to drop hints that foreshadow dangers ahead. You can show characters lying and misleading other characters. Or you can make characters give themselves away.

❻ Evoke emotion

Go back to the *Dinosaur Summer* extract on page 45. The author Greg Bear (left) says a lot about the characters here. He tells us about Peter's life and his relationship with his mother. If you tried to write all this information as a piece of narrative, it would probably be three times as long. His short answers also suggest caution borne from experience. There is a hint of Anthony's contempt for his ex-wife's mollycoddling. But it's Peter's sad little 'Oh' that makes us sympathize with him.

Now it's your turn

Talking with the enemy?

Write a short piece of dialogue between a human and an alien. One of them is pleading for his life. Decide whose point of view you are writing from. Try to find ways of indicating why one wants to exterminate the other. Make it humorous if you want to. Try to make the characters sound different from each other – an alien will not have the same speech patterns as a human even if they are speaking a common language. When you have finished, write the same thing as a piece of straight narrative, including the same information. Which version is the more interesting to read?

❼ Make your characters sound different to you

It is tempting to devise very strange words for your alien characters to speak, using strings of consonants or odd punctuation. Avoid doing this. It is difficult for the eye to unravel and if readers keep stumbling over strange words, they will stop reading and your story will have failed, no matter how good it was otherwise.

❽ Suggest language differences

You can make your characters sound different by small touches done sparingly. Devise a greeting, such as Mr Spock's 'Live long and prosper' in *Star Trek*, or some catchwords or phrases, that occur naturally in their remarks. Also non-native English speakers often speak in a more formal way. Compare 'It's my arm! You've broken it!' to 'It is my arm! You have broken it.'

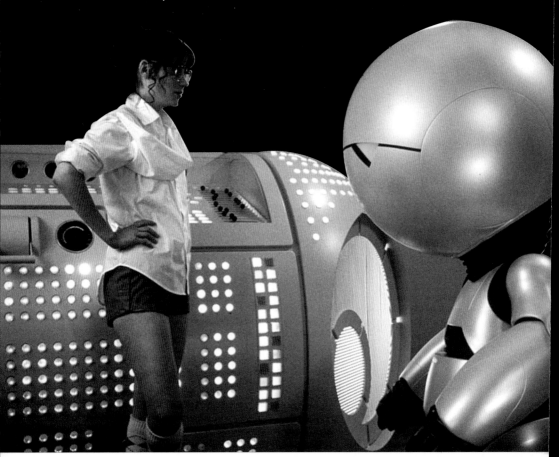

Now it's your turn

Family talk

Write down a typical conversation between you and one of your parents. Try to capture exactly how they speak. What words or phrases do they habitually use that are different from yours? Re-write it with a grandparent or elderly aunt speaking. Are there more differences?

⑨ Invent language

There are, of course, always writers who push the boundaries. Ursula K. Le Guin uses her upbringing in Indian cultures, and the knowledge of several languages to create a mythic way of speaking for the characters of her speculative worlds.

⑩ Use different accents

In Douglas Adams' *Hitchhiker's Guide to the Galaxy*, the two-headed Zaphod's hip way of speaking is caught in the following line: "Hey Earthman? You hungry kid?" said Zaphod's voice.

⑪ Keep in character

In *The Hitchhiker's Guide to the Galaxy*, Marvin the Paranoid Android (left) has such a well-drawn character that you always know when he is speaking:

> *"You think you've got problems," said Marvin as if he was addressing a newly occupied coffin, "what are you to do if you are a manically depressed robot? No, don't bother to answer that, I'm fifty thousand times more intelligent than you and even I don't know the answer. It gives me a headache just trying to think down to your level."*
>
> Douglas Adams, *The Hitchhikers Guide to the Galaxy*

TIPS AND TECHNIQUES

Dialogue will reveal lots of differences between the speakers, such as in age, education, intelligence, where they are from, etc. It will also give clues to the speakers' relationship, e.g. whether they are friends or foes.

BEATING WRITER'S BLOCK

Learning to write has ups and downs, and even famous writers get stuck. This is called writer's block. If you have been sticking to the writer's golden rule (page 9), writing often and brainstorming, then you already have some powerful weapons to combat this demon.

❶ Get over your insecurities

Whenever your internal critic looms on your brain scanner, do a timed brainstorming exercise to cut it down to size. Write something positive: about your favourite things or a great moment in your life. The more you do this, the more you will build up your writer's power – just like Luke Skywalker learning to wield his light sabre.

❷ Make writing a habit

To be a writer you must learn the writing habit. Write regularly – letters, emails, diary entries all count – and learn to write when you don't feel like it. Whenever you do a timed brainstorming session – even if it is only two minutes, you prove you can write.

❸ Coping with criticism

No one enjoys rejection or criticism, but it is an important part of learning to be a writer. If you invite someone to read your stories, you have to prepare yourself for negative comments. As you develop your writing skills, you will develop faith in yourself and your storytelling skills. Try to see criticism as a chance to make your story better – or maybe you just let the wrong person read it.

Now it's your turn

Positive thinking

Write on the cover of your notebook: WRITING IS OUT OF THIS WORLD. BUT IT'S NOT ALWAYS EASY!

Now brainstorm for five minutes, listing all the things you find difficult about writing. Repeat the exercise, only this time list all the things you love about writing. Now look over the problems. Are these things that can be fixed with more time and practice and a lot more reading? Is learning to write more important to you than the problems? If the answer is 'yes', then give yourself five gold stars. You are still heading towards a successful mission.

❹ Find fresh ideas

There are other causes of writer's block. One is believing that you have nothing to write about. But now you know that ideas are everywhere. The trick is to stop panicking and sit quietly. Any of the exercises in this book could help you find some new ideas. Or watch your favourite Sci-Fi shows. Don't try to copy them – that would be plagiarism – but use the plots or characters to inspire ideas of your own.

❺ Don't get stuck

It can be very depressing getting stuck half way through your story, but if it happens, it is often because you haven't thought the story out properly. Some vital ingredient is missing and the best way to find it is to go back to your story map (see page 33). Or simply leave this story for a while, and start something new. All stories have their natural time to emerge.

SYNOPSES & PLOTS | WINNING WORDS | SCINTILLATING SPEECH | HINTS & TIPS | FINISHING TOUCHES | WHAT NEXT?

❻ Understanding writer's block

The kind of writer's block that leaves you stuck usually means you have not done enough planning. If you have been following the exercises you will already know how to escape some of these black holes. One way to sort out a story block is to play a 'What If' game. Remember the android exercise on page 15. Try asking some new questions to help you create this character in more detail. For example, 'What if I confided my secret in my best friend? What if she told someone else and the whole school discovered? What if they all turned against me?' See how the questions build into a possible storyline.

❼ Rebuild your characters

If your key character isn't coming to life, turn your writing problem into a game with friends or family. You'll need a large sheet of paper. Sit in a circle and you start. In two minutes, write a brief description of your hero at the top of the paper. Pass it on and let the next person add their thoughts to yours, and so on round the circle. When the suggestions return to you, you may see your hero in a whole new light.

❽ Role Play

Try composing a group story. Have 12 or more scraps of paper. Write a character idea on each one, and drop them into a hat. Everyone chooses a character randomly and must be responsible for developing that character and weaving them into the story. Take it in turns to make story suggestions.

There are two rules: speak your first thoughts, and don't mind if others improve on your ideas. The end result should be like a chapter synopsis.

❾ Keep a journal

If you run out of things to write at practice time, start a diary. Write about life at school, home, record all the details of your hobbies and interests. Set yourself a minimum target for each entry, say 300 words or half a page. If you use a computer for writing, you can count them easily. Make a note. That way you can prove that you are working really hard.

Now it's your turn

Breaking down resistance

If you still think you have absolutely nothing to say, try this. Give yourself ten minutes to describe the most boring, mind-numbing thing you can think of. Say exactly why you find it boring and in the most telling words possible. Say how you survived the experience. Or maybe you didn't. Maybe it turned you into some other life form that just pretends to be you. Be funny, melodramatic, or downright ridiculous. Write it to entertain your friends.

TIPS AND TECHNIQUES

You won't run out of ideas if you keep reading. But remember to write them down in your notebook. If all else fails walk the dog, clean out your bedroom. Doing tasks that give your mind a rest could be just the way to spring an idea.

PREPARING YOUR WORK

When your finished story has been 'resting' for a few weeks, it is time to revise and edit it. After the break you will be able to see it with fresh eyes and spot any flaws more easily.

❶ Editing

Reading your work aloud will help you to simplify rambling sentences and correct dialogue that doesn't flow. Underline words that seem weak and replace them with stronger ones – 'dashed' instead of 'went', 'soared' instead of 'flew'. Cut words like 'very' and 'really' and remove unnecessary adjectives. Check your dialogue. Does it sound right? Would a Martian really say 'whatever'?

❷ Think of a title

It is important to think of a really good title – something intriguing and eye-catching that suggests the future. Think about some titles you know.

❸ Be professional

When you are absolutely happy with your story, write it out afresh, or type it up on a computer. This is your manuscript. If you have a computer, you can word process your manuscript and give it a professional presentation.

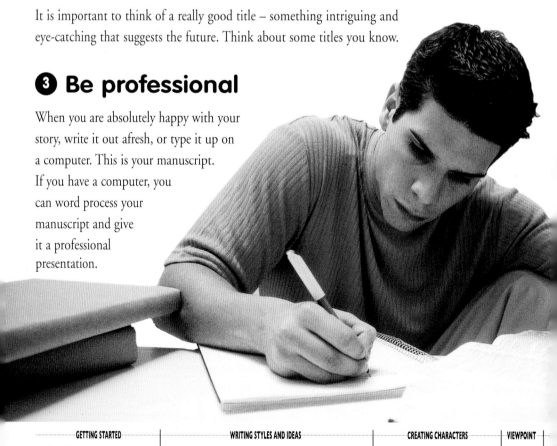

Manuscripts should always be printed on one side of A4 white paper, with wide margins and double line spacing. Pages should be numbered, and new chapters should start on a new page. You can also include your title as a header on the top of each page. At the front, you should have a title page, with your name, address, telephone number and email address on it.

❹ Make your own book

If your school has its own publishing lab, you could use it to 'publish' your own story or to make a class story anthology (collection). A computer will let you choose your own font (print style) and justify the text (making even length margins like a professionally printed page). When you have typed and saved your story to a file, you can edit it quickly with the spell- and grammar checker, or move sections of your story around using the 'cut and paste' facility, which saves a lot of rewriting. Having your story on a computer file means you can print a copy whenever you need one, or revise the whole story if you want to.

❺ Design a cover

Once you are happy with your story, print it out. You could then consider using the computer to design a science-fiction cover. A graphics program will let you scan and print your own artwork, or download ready-made graphics. Alternatively you could use your own digital photographs and learn how to manipulate them on screen to produce some highly original images. You can use yourself or friends as 'models' for your story's heroes.

TIPS AND TECHNIQUES

Whether you type up your story on a computer or do it by hand, ALWAYS make a copy before you give it to anyone else to read. If they lose your only copy, you will have lost all your precious work!

❻ Some places to publish your story

The next step is to find an audience for your science-fiction work. Family members or classmates may be receptive. If you are really ambitious you may want to get your work published via a publishing house or online site. There are several magazines and a number of writing websites that accept stories and novel chapters from young writers. Some give writing advice. Several run regular competitions. Each site has its own rules about submitting work to them, so make sure you read them carefully before you send in a story. See page 62 for more details. You can also:

• Send stories to your school magazine. If your school doesn't have a magazine, start your own with like-minded friends!

• Keep your eyes peeled when reading your local newspaper or magazines. They might be running a writing competition you could enter.

• Check with local museums and colleges. Some run creative-writing workshops during school holidays.

❼ Writing clubs

Starting a writing club or critique group and exchanging stories is a great way of getting your science-fiction story out there. It will also get you used to criticism from others, which will prove invaluable in learning how to write. Your local library might be kind enough to provide a forum for such a club.

Case study

Ursula K. Le Guin's award-winning book *The Left Hand of Darkness* was rejected by an editor as being 'unreadable' and the action 'hopelessly bogged down'. Ms Le Guin now posts it on her website as an encouragement to other writers who have received rejection letters. Her advice is '*Hang in there!*'

❽ Finding a publisher

Secure any submission with a paperclip and always enclose a short letter (saying what you have sent) and a stamped, addressed envelope for the story's return. Study the market and find out which publishing houses are most likely to publish science fiction. Addresses of publishing houses and information about whether they accept submissions can be found in writers' handbooks. Bear in mind that manuscripts that haven't been asked for, or paid for by a publisher – unsolicited submissions – are rarely published.

❾ Writer's tip

If your story is rejected by an editor, don't despair! See it as a chance to make the story better and try again! And remember; having your work published is wonderful, but it is not the only thing. Being able to make up stories is a gift, so why not give yours to someone you love? Read it to a younger brother or sister, or tell it to your grandfather. Your friends are also a ready-made audience.

TIPS AND TECHNIQUES

READ, READ, READ,
WRITE, WRITE, WRITE.
It's the only writing trick you will ever need.

WHEN YOU'VE FINISHED YOUR STORY

Finishing your first story is a brilliant achievement. You have created something entirely new, proved you can write and probably learned a lot about yourself too. So put your story aside for a week or so, and start a new one.

❶ Time to brainstorm?

Perhaps while you were writing the first story, an idea started simmering in your mind. Perhaps you made a few notes in your 'ideas' file. Do those ideas still excite you? Go back to the start of this book and repeat some of the brainstorming exercises to help you develop the idea further. Series like *Star Trek* or *Animorphs* have a complete adventure in each book but the details of the main characters' lives runs on from book to book to keep the readers hooked.

❷ How about a sequel?

When thinking about your next work, ask yourself: 'Can I write a sequel and develop the story? Is there a minor character whose tale I'm burning to tell?' Science-fiction stories lend themselves to sequels and series, because the effort that goes into creating a speculative world is bound to throw up lots more ideas. Or what about writing a trilogy? These three-book stories mirror the beginning-middle-end priciple of a single story structure – but on a grander scale. Book one introduces the characters and their problems, book two develops the conflict, and book three has the climax and resolution of the story.

❸ A famous example

At the end of *Star Trek: The Lost Years*, J. M. Dillard finishes with the sad parting between Dr McCoy and Spock, but at the very last moment manages to slip in a hopeful little hint that could suggest more stories to come:

> *McCoy stood, surprised by the sudden tightness of his throat. "Goodbye, Spock. Take care."*
> *He watched as the Vulcan, a stark and lonely figure in black, walked out of the empty bar. And somehow, his heart refused to accept that this time was the last.*

J.M. Dillard, *Star Trek: The Lost Years*

analogy – suggesting similarities between one thing (or situation) and another quite different thing (or situation)

backstory – the history of people or events that happened before the actual story begins

blurb – publisher's description on a book jacket that persuades you to read the book

chapter synopsis – an outline describing briefly what is happening in each chapter

cliché – a worn-out idea/description/plot, e.g. 'white as snow' is a cliché

cliffhanger – ending a chapter or switching viewpoint stories at a nail-biting moment

commission – when a publisher asks you to write a book for them

editing – removing all unnecessary words from your story and making it the best it can be

editor – the person who works in a publishing house and finds new books to publish. They also advise authors on how to improve their storytelling methods by telling them what needs adding or cutting

first-person viewpoint – stories told in the first person and describing only what that person experiences, e.g. 'It was July when I left for Timbuktu. Just the thought of going back there made my heart sing.'

foreshadowing – dropping hints of coming events or dangers that are essential to the outcome of the story

genre – a particular type of writing, e.g. fantasy, historical, adventure, science fiction are all examples of different genres

imagery – making word pictures. See also metaphor and simile

internal critic – the voice inside your head that picks holes in your work and makes you want to give up writing

light relief – a scene of lighter or humorous mood used to give readers a rest from too much suspense/action/drama

list – the list of book titles that a publisher has already published or is about to publish

manuscript – your story when it is written down, either typed or by hand

metaphor – calling a man 'a mouse' is a metaphor. It is a word picture. From it we learn in one word that the man is timid or pathetic, not that he is actually a mouse.

motivation – the reason why a character does something

narrative – adjective: telling the story; noun: the story

omniscient viewpoint – the all-seeing eye that sees all the characters and tells readers how they are acting and feeling

plagiarism – copying someone else's work and passing it off as your own; it is a serious offence

plot – the sequence of events that drives a story forwards

point of view (POV) – the eyes through which a story is told

sequel – a story that carries an existing one forward

simile – saying something is like something else. It is a word picture, e.g. clouds like frayed lace

speculative fiction – science fiction and fantasy that set stories in created worlds

synopsis – a short summary that describes what a story is about and introduces the main characters

theme – the main idea that is explored in the story such as war or slavery, or human values such as courage and justice. A story may have several themes.

third-person viewpoint – stories told in the third person, which only show events from that character's viewpoint

treatment – a brief summary of what a film is about, similar to a synopsis

unsolicited submission – sending a book or story to a publishers without being asked. These submissions usually end up in the slush pile

writer's block – when writers think they can no longer write

You can learn a lot from famous science-fiction writers' websites. Greg Bear's is www.gregbear.com. Robert J. Sawyer gives lots of advice about science-fiction writing on www.sfwriter.com. Use a computer search engine to locate your favourite authors' official sites.

Asimov's Science Fiction is a magazine with a great site at www.asimovs.com, and *Fantasy and Science Fiction* is at www.sfsite.com/fsf/

For general writing advice see author Aaron Shepherd's site: www.aaronshep.com/storytelling/

The Listen and Write site on the BBC website is all about writing poetry, but there are lots of fun exercises with rap, similes and freeform verse that will make all your written words sparkle: www.bbc.co.uk/eduction/listenandwrite/home.htm

Ask for a subscription to magazines such as *Cricket* and *Cicada* for your birthday. Or find them in your library. They publish the very best in young people's short fiction and you can learn your craft and read great stories at the same time. *Cicada* also accepts submissions from its subscribers. www.cricketmag.com/

Make a good friend of your local librarian. They can direct you to useful sources of information that you might not have thought of. They will also know of any published author scheduled to speak in your area.

Get your teacher to invite a favourite author to speak at your school. Many authors do schools' visits and workshops.

Places to submit your science fiction

The magazine *Stone Soup* which accepts stories and artwork from 8- to 13-year-olds. Their website is *www.stonesoup.com*

The Young Writers Club – an Internet-based club where you can post your stories. Check them out at:
http://www.csbilkent.edu.tr/~david/derya/ywc.html.
Or *Potluck Children's Literary Magazine* at *http://members.aol.com/potluckmagazine*

Young Writer at *www.mystworld.com/youngwriter/* and other similar sites at *www.kidauthors.com* for 6- to18-year-olds

www.kidpub.org/kidpub – a subscription club that posts 40,000 young people's stories 'from all over the planet'

Works quoted or mentioned in the text

The Hitchhiker's Guide to the Galaxy,
Douglas Adams, Pan 1979

Animorphs: In the Time of Dinosaurs,
K. A. Applegate, Scholastic 1998

Playing on the Edge,
Neil Arksey, Puffin 2000

Dinosaur Summer,
Greg Bear, Warner Books 1998

Vernon Bright and the Faster Than Light Show,
Steve Barlow & Steve Skidmore, Puffin 2001

Peacemaker,
Malorie Blackman, in *Fantastic Space Stories*
collected by Tony Bradman, Corgi 1995

Ender's Game,
Orson Scott Card, Atom 2002

"Encounter at Dawn",
Arthur C. Clarke in *Oxford Alien Stories*, ed. by
Dennis Pepper, Oxford University Press 2002

Star Trek: The Lost Years,
J. M. Dillard, Pan 1990

The City of Ember,
Jeanne DuPrau,
Doubleday 2004

Shadow of the Minotaur,
Alan Gibbons, Pearson Longman 2000

Dreamweaver,
Louise Lawrence, Collins 1996

Gathering Blue,
Lois Lowry, Bloomsbury 2000

Oxford Alien Stories, Dennis Pepper,
Oxford University Press 2002

Jumpman,
James Valentine, Corgi 2002

Flight for Freedom,
Sue Welford, 1994 in *Fantastic Space Stories*
collected by Tony Bradman, Corgi 1995

Predator's Gold,
Philip Reeve, Scholastic Point, 2004

The War of the Worlds,
H. G. Wells, *Science Fiction Stories*,
chosen by Edward Blishen, Kingfisher 1991

The Day of the Triffids,
John Wyndham, Penguin 1951

A

beginnings 23, 36–37

brainstorming 10, 13, 17, 21, 58

C

characters 24–29, 44, 48, 52

'classics' 34

cover design 55

criticism 50

D

dialogue 44–49

E

editing 54, 60

endings 32, 38, 40–41

G

getting started 8–13

glossary 60

H

heroes 24–29, 38

hints and tips 50–53, 57

I

ideas 14–23, 51

imagery 42, 60

inspiration 34

J

journals (diaries) 53

L

landscapes 20–21, 22

language 48–49

M

magical companions 29

middles 38–39

momentum 46

moods 43

N

names 25

novels or short stories? 35

O

openings 23, 36–37

P

places to write 8–9

plots 32–41, 61

points of view 30–31, 46, 60, 61

publishers 55, 56, 57, 62

R

reading habit 12–13, 57

research 18–19

rewarding yourself 11

rhythm 43

S

sci-fi meaning 12

sequels 58–59, 61

settings 20–21, 22

short stories or novels? 35

speech 44–49

story maps/webs 33, 35

styles 14–23

synopses 32–41, 61

T

themes 13, 34, 61

threat creation 23

titles 54

training 10

V

viewpoint 30–31, 46, 60, 61

villains 26–27

W

weaknesses 39

writer's block 50–53, 61

writer's experiences 6–7

writer's voice 14–15

writing materials 8

Picture Credits: Art Archive: 8b, 9t, 10t & b, 18-19c, 24t, 41t, 43b, 51t, 57cl, 23b, 32t 33 all, 38-39c, 39b, 57t, 58t, 58b. Corbis RF: 6-7 all, 12 all, 14-15 all, 16t, 17b, 29t, 30 all, 34c, 35t, 40t. Creatas: 4t, 19t, 28t, 42-43c, 48t, 49t, 52t, 54 all, 58b. Fotosearch: 16-17c, 30-31c, 43b, 44t, 50t, 56t and b, 62t. NASA: 8t, 18t, 59b. Rex Features: 1, 3, 5t, 9b, 10-11c, 13 all, 17t, 20-21 all, 22 all, 23t, 24b, 25 all, 26-27 all, 28t, 29t, 32c, 36-37 all, 38b, 40t, 42t, 44b, 45, 46b, 48-49c, 50c, 51c, 52b, 53c and 63, 53r, 55 all, 59tr, 60. Science Photo Library: 38t, 41b, 49b.